<u>E</u>

<u>Everyone</u> can coach kickers

or <u>teach themselves</u> to kick,

using the mechanics and drills,

I have described in this book.

Just follow my training philosophy:

<u>Training Philosophy</u>

Do each repetition **right**…..
do each repetition with **intensity**….
or…..
do each repetition **again**.

Coach Bill Renner

"**_Skills_ are different than _drills_.**

Drills develop proper mechanics.

Skills train mechanics for performance."

Coach Bill Renner

At-the-Upright Skill
Core Kicking Skill 1

Purpose: to develop the loading of the leg
to develop energy transfer in the accelerator foot
to develop body posture at ball contact
to develop hip acceleration at ball contact
to train foot-ball contact
to develop proper leg swing path
to train a "==*ball-striking*==" mindset

Mindset
The mindset needed to be a successful kicker is to be a "==*great ball-striker*==". How well you can strike the ball <u>where it needs to be</u> with the <u>right body position</u> is the determinant to how high, straight and far the ball will fly.

==*Ball-striking.*== Focus your attention. Make it your only goal. Use this as your only definition of success, <u>to hit slow tumbling, high, straight kicks</u>. This single mindset will enable you to hit better kicks more often.

Key to Consistent Ball Flight
Your leg acceleration at ball contact is important. Your foot being flat is important. Your finishing your leg swing is very important. Your knee inside the ball at contact is important. But <u>nothing is more important</u> than having your body "==*tall and behind the ball*==" at contact.

The ball will never be contacted perfectly every time. But you must have a technique that allows for success despite errors in ball striking. This is it.

*As long as you stay <u>tall with your upper body</u>,
and keep your <u>shoulders behind the ball</u> at contact,
you will be able to make an <u>ascending, accelerating swing</u>
which allows you to make consistent contact with the ball.*

If your upper body is in front of the ball at contact, your leg swing flattens and the ball comes out low.

If the your upper body crunches, shoulders slump down at ball contact, your leg swing decelerates at contact.

In both scenarios, your leg swing path and leg speed are affected and a less than ideal ball strike happens.

At-the-Upright Skill Tempo
This is not a full speed leg swing skill. It is a ½ - ¾ speed leg swing drill. The concept is to go at a speed that allows you to make perfect contact with the ball. Then, do the drill faster. Always start at a moderate speed and build up.

Going slower allows you to see the ball longer and to hold your body in the right ball contact position. These two things are more important in the drill than going fast.

We are training a skill not performing so the tempo needs to be a "training tempo" which is ½ - ¾ speed.

At-the-Upright Skill Setup
Tee the ball up 15 yards away from and directly across from one of the goal post uprights. Use a no step technique for this drill. Load your leg while maintaining upper body balance. Swing through to contact the ball.

The goal is to hit the upright with the ball. This tells you that your leg swing at ball contact was perfectly square and the leg swing after ball contact was right on the target line. This is not as easy as it seems.

At-the-Upright Skill Mechanics
Use a no step approach. Hold your body stable, tall and balanced. Load your kicking leg behind your back to initiate your leg swing.

Do NOT LEAN forward
to load your leg behind your body.

Make sure there is hip rotation when you load your leg behind your back and not just pulling your leg straight back.

As you load your leg:

- stand tall with your upper body,
- keep your non-kicking knee bent in athletic position
- keep your weight on the ball of your foot
- focus your laser eyes on your ball contact spot.

As you start your leg swing:

- point your knee at the ball contact spot
- keep your toe depressed for a flat foot contact surface
- snap and extend the knee at ball contact
- stay tall and behind the ball at ball contact
- finish square and balanced

At-the-Upright Skill Ball Flight Feedback
Watch each kick for flight feedback. If the ball does not hit the upright or is not within 1 yard to either side of the upright then you were not square to the ball with your foot at ball contact.

If the ball is to the right of the upright, you contacted the ball too early in your swing. Make sure you don't lean with your upper body to start your swing. Or, move your non-kicking foot back an inch or two.

<u>If the ball is to the left of the upright</u>, your swing started behind the ball and came across it, an outside-in path, at contact. Keep your knee inside the ball and contact the inside panel. <u>Think about going up into the ball at contact from the inside</u> not directly behind the ball.

Ball Contact Body Position Techniques

- tall at the ball
- body behind the ball
- laser eyes focused on the ball spot
- toe depressed for flat foot contact surface
- knee inside the ball spot

- stable upper body throughout the swing and at finish
- a perfect balanced swing that allows you to control ball flight
- body control equals ball flight control

At-the-Upright Skill
Core Kicking Skill 1

-stand 15 yards directly across from a goal post upright

if there is no goal post upright find a tree, light pole, etc. that is about 30 feet high

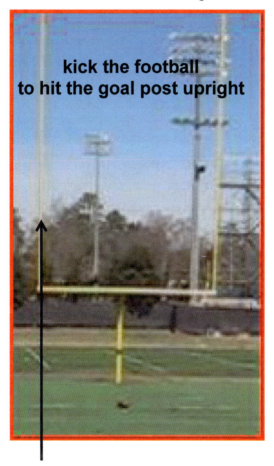

Kicker

-tee the ball up 15 yards directly across from the goal post
-use a no step technique
-stay "*tall and behind the ball*" at contact
- kicks should either hit the upright
or miss within a yard to either side
-height of the kick should be 1/3 of the way up the upright

Over-the-Upright Skill
Core Kicking Skill 2

Purpose: to develop the position of the accelerator foot, non-kicking foot, for ball contact
to develop a consistent rotation of the hips
to develop energy transfer from accelerator foot to hips, to foot-ball contact
to develop a smooth, rhythmical, consistent leg swing tempo

Mindset
You must be able to accelerate up into the ball to achieve height on kicks. Focus on a leg swing path that is *"inside and up"* into the ball. Visualize a ball flight path that is going above the upright. Recapture this thought at the moment of ball strike and this will enable you to stay inside and up into the ball. Think about finishing your swing so that your kicking foot would touch the top of the upright and this will assist in the path you need to accelerate up into the ball.

Over-the-Upright Skill Tempo
This is not a full speed skill. It is a ¾ speed skill. The concept is to go at a speed that allows you to hit 5 consecutive balls over-the-upright. Then, do the skill faster. Always start at a moderate speed and build up.

Going slower allows you to see the ball longer and to hold your body in the right ball contact position. These two things are more important in the drill than going fast.

We are <u>training a skill</u> not performing so the tempo needs to be a "training tempo" which is ¾ speed.

Over-the-Upright Skill Setup
Stand at the <u>intersection of the end line and the side line</u> and face the goal post upright. This will put you 23 yards from the upright. The top of the goal post will be used as the height target. <u>You want to kick the ball so that it rises above the top of the goal post</u> **before** <u>it gets to the goal post or as it passes the goal post.</u>

Use the goal post to continue to monitor the "at-the-upright" mechanics from the previous skill. This means you are trying to <u>keep the ball flight in line with the goal post as it goes above it</u>.

Over-the-Upright Skill Mechanics
Focus your attention on <u>staying tall and behind the ball at ball contact.</u> When you do this you will notice your shoulders have a downward tilt toward the ball at ball contact.

The <u>shoulders must remain stable and not moving during the leg swing</u> to direct all the body energy "==up==" into the ball for height.

<u>Use the one-step approach for this skill</u>. This teaches you to use your hips and leg snap acceleration to generate the speed to kick the ball over-the-upright. You must be <u>stable with your non-kicking leg and not move your upper body</u> as you rotate and accelerate the hips up and into the target.

*If your kick does not get consistent height
then your leg swing path is too much <u>rotational or circular</u> and
not <u>linear or vertical enough</u>.*

Rotational Swing Path
Load   Follow Through

Linear Swing Path
Load   Follow Through

Rotational swings have a lower leg load position and finish with a lower follow through. This is reflected in a lower ball flight.

Linear swings have a more vertical leg load position and descends steeper and ascends steeper on the follow through causing greater ball height.

Monitor the leg swing mechanics for the proper swing path and an aggressive acceleration of the hips up into the ball. The main purpose of this drill is to synchronize those two techniques.

Over-the-Upright Ball Flight Feedback
Watch each kick for ball flight feedback. Watch for the kick to travel over top of, above, the upright. This indicates that the leg swing path was right and the swing acceleration "up" into the ball was right too.

Monitor the kick for accuracy, the ball needs to travel over-the-upright and within a yard to either side. Use the *At-the-Upright* coaching tools described in the previous section to fix accuracy issues.

Leg Load Position   **Leg Swing Finish**

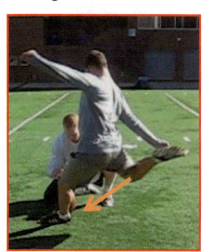 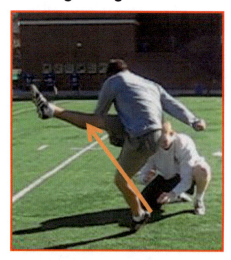

Over-the-Upright Skill
Core Kicking Skill 2

-stand on the endline and sideline facing an upright

if there is no goal post upright find a tree, light pole, etc. that is about 30 feet high

23 yards from the goal post upright or object

Kicker

-use a full 2-step approach
- slow down the approach process, go ¾ speed
-be a great ball striker
-kick 5 balls in a row that go over top of the upright

Down-the-Sideline Skill
Core Kicking Skill 3

Purpose: to develop the kicking specific muscles
                 to develop the kicker's stepping pattern
                 to develop the coordination of the kicking motion
                 to develop a fast and balanced leg swing

Mindset
You must be able to align the same way every time to have the same leg swing. Approach distance, lateral distance, stance body angle and path to the ball all must be honed to be exactly the same to reproduce a similar leg swing. Narrowing the target while working on this achieves a more focused, directed mindset.

Down-the-Sideline Skill Tempo
This is not a full speed skill. It is a ¾ speed skill. The concept is to go at a speed that allows you to hit 5 consecutive balls between the goal posts and over the uprights. Then, do the skill faster. Always start at a moderate speed and build up.

Going slower allows you to see the ball longer and to hold your body in the right ball contact position. These two things are more important in the drill than going fast.

> *We are training a skill not performing so the tempo needs to be a "training tempo" which is ¾ speed.*

Down-the-Sideline Skill Setup
Stand on the sideline at the goal line on the right sideline. Position the ball so that you are kicking at the goal posts. After 3 kicks from this position, move 3 yards "down-the-sideline" into the end zone and kick 3 kicks.

Then move 3 more yards "down-the-sideline" into the end zone (6 yards deep now) and kick 3 more kicks. Finally, move 3 yards more (now 9 yards deep in the end zone) and kick 3 final kicks. Repeat this from the other sideline.

Down-the-Sideline Skill Mechanics
Using your full approach steps, kick the football through-the-goal posts and over-the-upright. The angle created by standing on the sideline to kick through the goal post narrows the goal posts so you have to kick through a smaller target.

This demands that your alignment, approach distance, lateral distance, stance body angle and path to the ball be next to perfect to make it through the narrower target.

Focus your thoughts on being balanced and square at contact, keeping your leg moving toward the goal posts after contact, and finishing balanced. These are the essentials of being a great ball striker and controlling ball flight.

Swing full speed.

Avoid making a conservative or tentative swing. This may subconsciously happen because with the narrow target a tendency is to want to guide the ball instead of swinging full speed at it.

Down-the-Sideline Ball Contact Flight Reads
Watch the ball flight for feedback on technique corrections. If the ball does not go between the goal posts or over the top of the uprights:

Decelerating at ball contact causes a pushed kick. It has a straight ball flight that just misses to the kicking leg side of the goal post. Correct this by rotating your hips aggressively to the target.

Outside-in leg swing path causes a pulled kick. It has a hook or curved ball flight to the opposite side of your kicking leg.

Think "*inside and up through the ball*". When you swing up through the ball it reduces the rotation of the swing across the body. This is what causes the "*outside-in*" swing path..

*Accelerating up through the ball at contact,
keeps the ball on the target line longer
and helps to overcome mishit kicks.*

Those mishits will now have enough linear momentum to make it through the goal post even if they don't look pretty.

If the ball does not go above the upright then generally our leg load and leg swing are too flat. Stay tall and load the leg by pulling your heel to a vertical position then descend to the ball and ascend up into the ball.

Left Down-the-Sideline View
From 5 yards deep into the End Zone

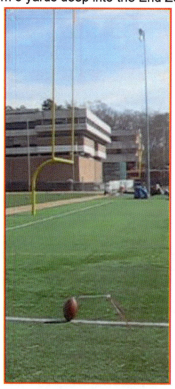

Right Down-the-Sideline View
From the Goal Line and Sideline

5 yards deep more narrow target   Wider target on Goal line/Sideline

Notice the difference in the goal post width when you move just 5 yards down-the-sideline.

Down-the-Sideline Skill
Core Kicking Skill 3

-stand on the Goal line and Sideline and face the goal posts

Right Down-the-Sideline View
From the Goal Line and Sideline

Left Down-the-Sideline View
From 5 yards deep into the End Zone

Position 1
Goal line and Sideline

Position 2
5 yards into the end zone

Procedures
-use a full 2-step approach
- slow down the approach process, go ¾ speed
and be a great ball striker
-kick 3 balls at each spot
- try to kick the ball through the goal posts
and over the goal posts

Hash Mark Field Goals
Core Kicking Skill 4

Purpose: to develop an alignment routine for each hash
to overcome visual effects of hash mark kicks
to learn that you never subconsciously master the hash mark kicks

Mindset
<u>Kicking from the left or right hash mark gives the kicker a different visual challenge.</u> Invariably, the angle effects of kicking from a hash mark become a nemesis for every kicker.

You must be able to align with slight adjustments when you are on a hash mark to have the same leg swing every time. <u>Approach distance</u>, <u>lateral distance</u>, <u>stance body angle</u> and <u>path to the ball</u> all must be monitored to overcome the visual hash mark challenge.

Hash Mark Field Goal Tempo
This is a full speed skill. <u>We want you to go at game speed once you move to kick the football.</u> Don't ease your way into the ball, swing at it full speed in control.

*We are working on a performance skill
so we need to go game tempo
to simulate game conditions.*

Hash Mark Field Goal Skill Setup
Start with the ball on the left hash on the 20 yard line for a 30 yard field goal. Kick one ball from here and then move backward 5 yards to the 25 yard line for a 35 yard field goal.

Repeat this moving backward every time until you have kicked 5 field goals from 30, 35, 40 42 and 45 yards.

Hash Mark Field Goal Mechanics

Left Hash Right Footed Kicker

Use your normal full approach steps. If you find that this approach and lateral distance allows the ball to fly at the uprights keep this alignment.

If you start pulling the ball to the left of the uprights make an adjustment with your lateral distance (stepping over to the side distance). **Add** a half step to your lateral or side over distance if you are pulling the ball.

Increase your side distance by ½ yard, if you are pulling your kicks from the left hash.

Right Hash Right Footed Kicker

Use your normal full approach steps. If you find that this approach and lateral distance allows the ball to fly at the uprights keep this alignment.

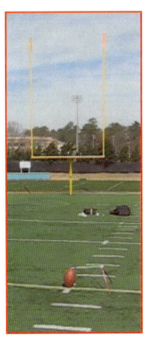

If you start pushing the ball to the right of the uprights make an adjustment with your lateral distance (stepping over to the side distance). **Subtract** a half step to your lateral or side over distance if you are pushing the ball.

Decrease your side distance by ½ yard, if you are pushing your kicks from the left hash.

From both hash marks, swing full speed. Avoid making a conservative or tentative swing. This may subconsciously happen because with the narrow target a tendency is to want to guide the ball instead of swinging full speed at it.

Hash Mark Field Goal Mechanics
Hash Mark Field Goal Ball Contact Flight Reads

Watch the ball flight for feedback to make technique and mindset corrections.

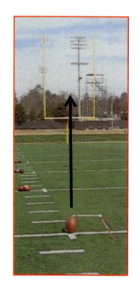

For a right footed kicker from the left hash, the target appears to be large and right in front of them. It is in a natural visual sight line. The kickers' tendency from the left hash is to be more proficient.

Misses usually come from hooks to the left because the kicker swings easier but with less precision resulting in an "outside-in" swing and a pull to the left.

For a right footed kicker from the right hash, the target is off to his left and is a visual challenge. He has to look back over his left shoulder to see the target after his alignment.

This visual cue can cause the kicker to overestimate the amount of rotation he needs to position his foot by the ball.

This over rotation creates a mindset that causes the kicker to want to avoid a big hook ball flight.

To avoid this he decelerates his swing and tries to guide the ball through the uprights instead of making a normal aggressive swing.

No one ever subconsciously masters the hash marks. It always requires conscious thoughts to avoid these two visual challenges. This is why Hash Mark Field Goals is one of the Core Kicking Skills.

Hash Mark Field Goals
Core Kicking Skill 4

Left Hash Field Goal View **Right Hash Field Goal View**

Procedures
-use a full 2-step approach
-kick balls from 30, 35, 40, 42 and 45 yards
- monitor your alignment to insure you can kick
5 straight balls at the middle of the goal posts

Training Guidelines For Kicking Skills

Training Sequence

Do this Skill Sequence 3 times a week

Monday, Wednesday, Friday

To develop ball flight control mechanics.

Skill	Sets	Repetitions	Goal
At-the-Upright	1	10	hit the goal post 3 times
Over-the-Upright	1	10	over the top of the goal post 5 times
Down-the-Sideline	1	5	goal line/sideline
	1	5	5 yds deep endzone
	1	5	8 yds deep endzone
Hash Mark Field Goals	1*	5	left hash field goals 30,35,40,42,45yds
	1*	5	left hash field goals 30,35,40,42,45yds

*try to make all 5 field goals in a row from each hash

QUICK FEET Kicking Drills
Coaching Points

1. **FULL Approach**
   a. Start 2 1/2 yds behind and 1 ½ yds over from the ball spot
   b. Put kicking foot forward with toe pointing at back of tee or spot
   c. Tall, athletic position, weight on ball of plant foot
   d. Push off non-kicking foot to get your body moving -"0-60mph BURST"
   e. On approach, pick feet up and down like "PISTONS" to generate leg speed and remain balanced and stable in upper body throughout approach
   f. Drive off the first step "ACCELERATE"
   g. Place plant foot in the box, toe straight at target
   h. Hit the ground with a heel-toe-UP off plant step
   i. Maintain <u>balance and posture</u> throughout the swing while going FULL SPEED
   j. Finish balanced-square to target, no leaning left, right or backward

2. **ONE Step Drill**
   a. Start 1 yd behind and 1 yd over from the spot of the ball
   b. Put kicking foot forward with toe pointing at back of tee
   c. Tall, athletic position, weight on ball of plant foot
   d. Drive off the first step "ACCELERATE"
   e. Place plant foot in the box, toe straight at target
   f. Hit the ground with a heel-toe-UP off plant step
   g. Maintain <u>balance and posture</u> throughout the swing while going FULL SPEED
   h. Finish balanced-square to target, no leaning left, right or backward

QUICK FEET Kicking Drills
Coaching Points

3. <u>NO Step Drill</u>
   a. Foot in "plant box"
   b. Tall, athletic position, weight on ball of plant foot
   c. Pull kicking foot off the ground remaining balanced and stable in upper body
   d. Pull kicking foot heel back to the butt cheek
   e. Transfer weight from heel to toe and push UP through the contact zone
   f. SNAP the kicking leg downward
   g. ACCELERATE through contact
   h. Finish balanced-square to target, no leaning left, right or backward

4. <u>FULL Kick Swings</u>
   a. Will contacting the ball change your mindset or mechanics?
   b. Be AGGRESSIVE and ATTACK the football
   c. Be a GREAT ball striker
   d. The FULL Kick mechanics should be the same as the FULL Approach
   e. Start 2 ½ yds behind and 1 ½ yds over from the ball spot
   f. Put kicking foot forward with toe pointing at back of tee
   g. Tall, athletic position, weight on ball of plant foot
   h. Push off non-kicking foot to get your body moving -"0-60mph BURST"
   i. On approach, pick feet up and down like "PISTONS" to generate leg speed and remain balanced and stable in upper body throughout approach
   j. Drive off the first step "ACCELERATE"
   k. Place plant foot in the box, toe straight at target
   l. Hit the ground with a heel-toe-UP off plant step
   m. Maintain <u>balance and posture</u> throughout the swing while going FULL SPEED
   n. Finish balanced-square to target, no leaning left, right or backward

Kicking Syllabus
Kicking Situations to Master

1) <u>Field Goals</u> (same as doing Line Drill)
    a. Left hash
    b. Right hash
    c. Middle

2) <u>Wet Field Field Goals</u>
    a. Middle -30 yd line *emphasize short, balanced steps = Quick Feet Drill position only slower

3) <u>Field Goals into the wind</u>
    a. Focus only on ball striking; field position is irrelevant

4) <u>Field Goals with the wind</u>
    a. Focus only on ball striking; field position is irrelevant

5) <u>Field Goals with a Left/Right crosswind</u>
    a. Focus only on ball striking; field position is irrelevant

6) <u>Field Goals with a Right/Left crosswind</u>
    a. Focus only on ball striking; field position is irrelevant

7) <u>Fake Field Goals</u>

8) <u>Kickoffs</u>
    a. Left hash
    b. Right hash
    c. Middle
    d. 50 going in
    e. +40 yd line
    f. -40 yd line

Kicking Syllabus
Kicking Situations to Master

9) <u>Directional Kickoffs</u>
    a. Directional Left
    b. Directional Right

10) <u>Onsides Kickoffs</u>
    a. High bounce Left
    b. High bounce Right
    c. Kicker surprise middle squib

11) <u>Sky Kickoffs</u>
    a. Left numbers
    b. Right numbers
    c. Middle to 3rd line

12) <u>Bombs Away</u>
    a. Right Hash -35 yd line (land inside the 10 yd line)
    b. Left Hash – 35 yd line (land inside the 10 yd line)
    c. Right Hash -40 yd line (land inside the 10 yd line)
    d. Left Hash -40 yd line (land inside the 10 yd line)

13) <u>Pre-Game Routine</u>

14) <u>Sideline Possession Warm-up</u>

15) <u>Bad Snap Field Goals</u>
    a. On ground, holder puts it down late
    b. High snap, holder puts it down late
    c. Reaching snap, holder crosses the spot
    d. High snap, holder does not get it down
    e. Low at the shins
    f. Skips back on the ground

16) <u>Grading Game Film</u>

For additional coaching educational materials

by Coach Bill Renner

visit:

www.billrennerfootball.com

Made in the USA
Lexington, KY
05 December 2015